It was a terrible cloud at twilight

. . . .

Contents

. . . .

III

It was a terrible cloud at twilight
· · · · · · · · · · · ·

Imposter

Imposter returned. Lighter than snowfall.
With her dangling mittens and fox-thin chin.
Came to the back porch by starlight.
Came in a clown's cap and a lopsided
ribbon. She had many guises, but you'd memorized
her track. Snow sprigged around her; the stars festooned,
then leaked into air—burning cold on burning
hot. She jazzed through and slid to ice—
that's how clear she was, how precise. Imposter made
war a kind of warmth. With a loose-fit grin,
shadows pacing her face. A rabbit lay dead
in her wake.

She Will

Because she loves you she will empty her linen drawers and fill
them with bluegrass   she will let you push her against the sill, loosening
her blouse   she will not object to blinking ceilings or yellow
petals in the basin   she will curse alongside you and greed
for beer in the blunt-mouthed bottle   she will gyrate in lunatic-fringed
dresses   she will croon raw and singularly, untie the hood of the bell,
and slip her fingers in   she will open her front and back door
for the ransacked wind   she will paint all walls in marigold, avocado,
violet, and rain   address swans as sovereignty and purple as god,
wear sundown hats and bless the stains you've pressed into
carpet and sheets   she will house a gangled field of dandelions
and drunken orioles   she will will herself to the broken clocktower
and again again she will hurl her silver body through ragged flames
and spear the light that spears   the wall she will make love to while
you watch from the rocking chair   she will crawl over the floor
panting, pretending to be the lioness you've always craved
and when the wild mane of night tames and curtains are drawn
your heart still beating loud with her changes, you will
whisper *where has she gone* and you will miss the shadowy her,
the one from before, while the one without shadow surrounds you
smoothing, stroking your skin, kissing your neck
down to the spine, down to where there is no turning back, to where you begin
to harden for her again.

First,

cat in estrus.
Next, gash.

A seam for a womb—.

Hung head,
awk. leg, off-placed
hip.

Low blue half-slinks

through the living room and slight tiger-
strip's unblinking eye

still won't blink
and then out of turn and bluntly I begin
to bleed

and he-who-was-my-lover leaves and shuts
the door even before

the cat's doped up and still
in pain, terse stitches over the shaved
belly and the listless list—.

After they sewed her
w/ whisker-string—
her dulling-dud, her new

non-yowling-hood.

Meditation on Fish

Some were spent arrows, blackly nosing forth while suspended.
Some, low blue globules
w/ slit flanks, gill-flower fins, petal-flaps,
whiskery, mad-eyed, stealthy undercover bullets,
noiseless breathers. They were dangerous, endangered.
Unblinking handfuls sleeking through water, tattery,
tiny wings fluttering beneath them
a little desperately, as if dropped
from the chipped sky, planetary outcasts.

I lived w/ their steadfast mass,
w/ their silver specks that didn't flick around
the bend, immune to the overhanging air
that would do them in. Perhaps it was reverie that kept them hanging
or some meditation guarding necessary shallows,
blunt-nosed sentinels of murk, stunning
their slighted faces against the imagined.

Nostalgia

The dark kicks up
its shimmer. Remember

when catch & fish
was a sentence,

glimmer took precedence
over lake

& burnish defied
the dull
skull, surpassing sheer bone?

(Scales sworn upon
glisten
& glint exiled by dry hook.)

Remember the emerald-eyed fly
& the glittering
leaves & river,

how autumn ambered
& the city glowed with steeples?

We lived then in a private cloud
with a powder-blue exterior
a white Cadillac interior
& the thin, gold smell of scotch—

I was the cracked-blue leaf & you
were a staggering sycamore, conducting
majestic night—*no no no*—

you made music
repeal itself until it got
too beat to stir

& I tapped the shore
incessantly
for the winged blade of word.

The Mice of the Mother's House

The mice of the mother's house had tiny faces and breathed
behind the paint, skittering like ticket stubs beneath
floorboards, light and anxious. A few had small subway-car
bodies tunneling fast, pushing roughshod over the grouting, nosing
the dust of their brothers' wake, cheeky, whiskery.
They loosed the interior wiring of the wall, their sharp eyes darting,
plaster-flecked, looking, for a moment, filled with snow.

In winter, the house swayed and shuddered with their
rustling. Hundreds of secret feet. One sped from under the piano
(gauntly hunched like an angel on all fours in its shiny black overcoat).
Mice-racket rocked the crystal chandelier. Mice-mildew
plumbed the good fixtures. Some veered back into the ice-
wrecked field with frozen, dirty mouths.

They were wounded by hammered nails, deafened by the brass
bull she hurled into the wall past the father's shaded face. The battery
of fists bellied their winding rooms, cracking their foyers. Their throats
filled with saw-scruff, grew dry and lost from crying
such little cries. From living hidden lives. Ringed by their brethren's
bodies and bones, gnawed corks. Ringed by what they had half-
chewed—the tattery fringe of the page.

Nothing she did derailed them. They snarled in wire, their
desiccate pink feet stiff like spokes, the little wheels
of their hearts awry. They lived overhead and beyond—
inaccessible, inviolate. Faintly panting in their closing cloud.

Icicles

Those brothers banged them till they fissured,
fell to snow. They used sticks or bats
or stones. Sometimes missed. Sometimes split
the glimmering to a shatter, a cough
of electric dust—the burning stickled
their skins. Those brothers said nothing
was good about them—they damaged the eaves
and dragged the house down—said they were
a poor excuse for rain or any form
of weeping, streaking through their freeze.
But I longed for them to stay, longed
for their elegance to last,
the tiny silver cities and gold
sea illumining their edges,
the slender bodies hanging
impeccably from the eaves, barely
hanging from anything. They were miracles,
their points dissolving in the smoldering
grip of a hand that could
end it all. Any hand.

Child of Fear:

By the bed that lies square
By the sky that lies shapeless

In a wrecked yellow forest
she is studying holes.

The bullet of solitude,
that faceless instructor,

bores through her skin, forming
dark portals from whatever it touches.

Under its tutelage, she is sister to wood-bee,
drilling dank shingles to dust.

Her tiny punctures make eye-
sockets for rain.

She takes an oath against planks,
outstacks cedar with absence-of.

The gypsy moth is her hoodlum leader—
together they infiltrate the grove.

(In thin air, the little dunes of debris
pile, whispering unintelligibly.)

There are endless parades of holes, the sky
is humming with holes, the earth collapsing
to dirt-frittered lace, as she

writes the book of unmaking.

Wolf

My owl was
a deadened petal. My moon
a leadweight hat.

Sinewy and sidelong, I
slowly circled, tail
bruised yellow,
a mouthful of splinters,
and skittery gunshy eyes

that met the skulking bullet
one spring and couldn't
fix again, didn't want to feed—

my brittle haunch arched thin, made
space for rattlesnakes to rise.
My shifty flank-bones,
driftwood in tired water.

Under the familiar
plummeting clouds,
in the vast, vulture-slow
terrain

(all west, all sinking)

I stopped claiming
the light

and hunkered off with rag-tag wing,
blood matting my chin, the dead croon
deep in my throat, the body
beside the point.

Trio from Blackwater Falls

the okay

Finally I gave myself permission to be
abstract. I shoveled off the leaf and rooster claw,
unhinged the maw of the autumn river
from my ankle—things of that nature. I stilled
myself to a cloud—portentous and opaque (what
we can't touch won't touch us)—then made myself missive—
an envelope. I couldn't bear the bulk, so thinned to glass—
invisible, hard, belonging both to the world
and to what stared back.

the cloud

and though it is hardly breathing
it's streaked violet
and ruffles through the sun's flame
and though its skin's mere as ribbon
stained by rain and though its troubled
vein took a wrong turn, and though it is
barely breathing, its mouth is infinite

resurrection

the bluebird house became a little ship
wind-wrecked, recoiling in the current—
the warped belly wouldn't hold a lick
of salt and there was more to the story—
bird-taps in the house without staircase,
without lantern, a delicate
tenement of unpacked boxes, musty brown,
peppery with dust, doors flapping
like a woman's sea-licked skirt as she stands on the cliff
yearning to be myth

Piece by Piece He Went
for Bill

First, his blue toe.
Then, his calf up to the hipbone.
He thinned to a frame.

Fireflies faltered, lit into
his bony lattice, the fretted ribs, mating
between collarbone and pelvis

till the whole leg fell off and inside
he was all air and brightness and treefrogs—

(bluethroated crickets struggled through his beard,
a meadow rose from the cave of his stomach)

—we tried to catch their tender bodies,
their thrumming hearts
that longed to be let back

into the wild yellow grass—no matter how
rotten with dew, no matter how
darkened by rain, no matter.

My Mother Raised Me to Be a Cowboy

Cause I was lonesome
for spur, dug
my naked heel
in glass. Cause I needed
clank, got my bones
thin and close to the hard world.

Cause I lost grasp of what was
smoke, shifty ghost-foots, thready
past, gripped the visible
moon-horn, turned leathern face
to the old-cat sun, clutched
the rope, jerked on the boot and saddled quick.

My cattleprod cramped a shadow.
My gaunt rifle ready for damage.
Got used to sleeping in bad spaces
snowed in with burlap.
Cause I was odd-eyed, hungered with wolves,
I yowling, bristled yellow like prairie.

Cause I ached for the stars, palomino
went lame. Cause I had no thought
to cry home, memorized the swagger,
hip-twist, slow smile. And mostly
my quiet was scorched. And most of my whiskey
drunk fast. Most of my sundowns forgot—

Most of the stare-downs stared off—
Most of the town killed to dust—
Most of the world smothered by hats—
Most tongues cut out—I spoke in grunts—
Most of the sky was mine.

Till the low hawk swung down.

II

In the Yard,

I am raking through stars—
Their faces, damp and yellow,
won't pick up.

I smell their tail-smoke
in the red oak, singed.
Its soft, tarnished arms
bothered by wind.

It was how many
pinned? How many stiffly
shot to harrowed dirt, blackly
pitting the earth?

In the pale aftermath,
the rain could not
tap music
into them. The moon could not
calculate, but dimly faced

the fading scarlet outcasts
in skinflint hats,
those wetted and gassed.

Low on the branch, low
on the rack, a few
freezing notices,

colorless maps—
not stars, not leaves—we rake
through—we hang back.

It was a terrible cloud at twilight,

humped painfully against
the last blast of light;
a threadbare wolf pressed in smoke;
a tyranny of doves on the outset pecking blindly white.

It was a terrible cloud—
everybody stared at its shifting instead of:
crumpled handfuls of animal below,
traffic lights, red beady ones, even yellow flashers,
green signs half-toppled, roofs slack with snow.

It was a terrible cloud—
isolated from sunset
and moon—on a furious sojourn.

The wind swerved
again and it was two thin bears in suits,
then men in gasoline-proof
jumpers, long arms flagging
like those in buildings ready to jump,
then uneasy triangles or angels, whatever
everybody would believe. The terrible cloud

could not contain
its mists, it split into a wispy
shepherd, a faint sketchy
hand trying to touch
a boulder impossible
to budge. When it blew

to a blur, the village
wishfully claimed it, warning
the world it was sinking.
Everybody hooked fingers
through tree-boughs, shadows,
stones, strangers. The bell

to itself thought: *How lost*
have lost; how many lost lost;
many passing through lost; lost
to themselves, everybody thought (but

they were in on it—
they wore the same smoke).

When You Ask

I am a red light
or a yellow car heading steadily
into blue
where the sad helium dwells—
risen, but fixed—
without memory of the village and animals
lying below it, without memory
of pulling through air a glowing balloon, something
the children loved.

I am a red light. My neighbor,
the fat dove, hangs
on snapping wire. Its mate
twig-entangled or part-blind or
flat-out gone. (I shine everything blood.)

Light or helium or dove we're
whistling like the charry train of memory—wistful, faint—
whistling as air does when it leaves.

I am hanging and clanking on my chain.
Look at me tenderly when you
say—wait tenderly for my reply—

I am a red light watching a yellow car drive into blue—
that distant—like a sun feeding
the world that is slowly
taking it down.

Flight___

A white line drops
out of the sky, a trailing cloud-
string, a quiver.

Was it a war, a plane's unintentional
scrape among hilly·scuds of smoke,
barely heard in the wire-stung sky?
Was it a death wherein death wants us for other

reasons, a day rolling when we don't want
to roll, wherein we gamble without sturdy eye, wherein
the petal's lost to its limited garden?

Both sides of the blue porch blue.
The porch lights damned dark.
Linnets and starlings stunned as if stuck on a high,
worried limb.

We were raised
to stare through wild birds in the cage, their start
at the bars, raised to stare down
the sky and the sea and the stars.

Infinity, if you can hear,
end at least with a little number.

One Day I Was Watching the Birds

The spit-polish grackles and the blackbirds with their bright razors
tucked in each wing, and the purple finch
disoriented, absent-minded,
a nuthatch-tuft nosing above the crammed yard—whirling dazedly,
near-sated, in full arcs around
the thin, pecked perch—the house wrens
gobbling seed, the slivered, empty shells rising
to hills of spackled dust.

They got fatter and fatter and more indiscriminate, drinking
water from the banged-out garbage lid, beaking
the house and its rusted gutter for shingle-grit—
chittering, vomiting husk.
Crows became suet-begotten bags on wings.
Bloat-plumaged sparrows lost their litheness. Lusterless sleeks pumping
dully in circles. What miracle or horror propelled them?

Their bellies aching as though empty
even after they'd had their fill, even after
their wings rammed
one into the other
until their little green tower of seeds cracked, fell, hemorrhaging
my squirrel-heart, flooding my rabbit-eye.

The Day the Lady Wore a Mask, a Bomb Strapped to Her Side

Above the Patron Saint of Steel
Above the Patron Saint of Coal
the east rose window roughed up the west rose window
till it went to shadow and light sped through
bulleting our sleeves
like paper, perforated,
then torn clean.
The crude, cold pews behind us
bolted in.

And in another room of the world,
below a basket's shattered net
on spit-polish yellow boards, canary-bright,
each too narrow to reflect a face,
children half-dressed by the heat
like undone coats slumped on the floor.

While a man drilled holes in the ceiling
with a gun
for adequate breath,
another, faceless, knelt
three inches from a huddled boy and pulled
out, beginning to unload.

The gymnasium of small flames and faint sweat
and those who wet
themselves made us forget
to consider the mosaics, the stained glass, and the last
saint we'd seen—Anthony in statuary, chinked robes,
his dear, stony eyes beholding
and unmet.

12 Stanzas on the Line

Tinsel and lace scuffle in the box
seeking bold bolts and tough swath.

Hands shift
like ornaments in a high ghostly wind.

Light breaks
a bell. The cold sky leaks.

Like gaslights, galaxies
blow out.

Trousers creep
off, unzipped.

Sleeves split day-
light in the chest.

Black tracks on bare thread
erupt in silent snow: buttons.

Hems off
the map, misplaced
geography.

Hours wait
for air to empty

into citadel, ditch, slip,
detonation, tuneless, nameless. Stop.

Waltz
of the three-legged gun, song
of bombstuffed lung.

Words, our pale matchstick children, hang
a bodiless wash.

When they said *wet T-shirts on at ten* at the motorcycle rally,

girls got tough breath, leaned in
and jut their hips, the stage shortened. Men
smoked murderous, angled shoulders out
like greasy crows with cock-eyed bellies,
their laughter quick and blunt with whiskey's
spike, slow-lidded eyes, cloud in the gleam, the lashes
like sticking lace dragged through mud. Then
a bare rump rose from the leathery creek, its oily
chains clandestine in rusty water. The dingy droop
of spruce by the banks did nothing to shade them. Boots cracked-in
and boots a knife cracked on and the air fell away
like tender meat as they say when they said *wet
T-shirts on at ten.* The girls' low grins stretched
and left little creases in their lipsticked lips, their powdery
faces like floating ghosts, but tight-eyed, they elbowed
each other in thin sides. They were used to this.
The other women hung back heavy in black leather
by the fry-smoke tents, near the jangling discs and dream-
webs—barely listening. What for. The music stopped. Everyone drunk.
Now them. And the T-shirts without arms hanging
for sale —all holes and glittering and black or pink and the ribs'
onerous turning on the fat-encrusted grill and the dull fume
of waiting for *wet T-shirts on at ten* filling the field, what was left
of it, beyond the gleaming rods and fetal engines,
coldblooded bars across the chest or bronze, those folded arms,
remnant of a father's approbation—curse, splatter, the trouble
starting up, the grunt, smack down cold to the ground
and the wet grass punished by booze and glass and ash—
for simply being underfoot. In the creek, one duck
pushed off fast. It had been a hot summer,
three boys found dead in a trunk, and the usual—*on at ten*—stripping
down what was already stark and plain and gone.

Worm-Wag in Magnolia Root

Love, the oak
is talking again
about the river that died in its head.

Love, the oak, the sycamore
stripped, the word
already spread about said
sycamore, but oak
has been a long-time yellow ribbon.

Love, the elms, the elms are at it again,
at it beyond acrid beetles,
above laurels' hooded nods, and rhododendron
(talk dry, talk fast, talk slow).
Twigs dropped here, but proud buds uphold.

Love, the forests, the forest again—
whisper of blue spruce,
sliding eternity of sassafras,
breach of beech, aborted birch—
a little glance the way
of the ant, a little slip
of worm-wag in magnolia root—

in burroway hills and frittered earth
and plangent moss with its small, stifled screams,
and concrete, the roofshed of our lives. Stop
toiling in crenellations (someone somewhere said)—
behold the dark graces in mudswallow swill—
reckon of rainbows, crimp-legged grass-hurdlers,
flowery ashes—our ghostly saviors of spring.

Love, the hurled cloud, oil-burled lash, evening—
the slickest slapdash alleyway of us and them and
you, love, needing safety in the end, the end worth
saving is.

On Balloons That Have Hissed Out

We were having a picnic when we found them.

Like abandoned petals
(pale magnolia choked and flushed, bursting in flustered bloom)
(dogwood petal unpacked from the dark trunk, freed from its floating
act to a yellow blister)
—one a silky blue ear
wilting on the hot-top tar
—one a cut-up cloud
that gave its last white gasp
—one a purple scab softened and bloated
by rain, peeled from its original skin.

These pieces were want-to-be sails
with their tiny muster—now
grounded after such short drifts of purposelessness
wherein they'd pressed up
the air, swell-headed and empirical—nodding
to the elms and helicopters and awnings and swings.

Remember all the air that put them there?
Remember the helium years
that filled their heads to a colorful bouquet
tossed up like giant roses and oversized carnations
at the matador-sky's cloaked face
at the ballerina-cloud's waxy poise
at the president of wind that must deadhead
anything thrown, any ecstatically flung thing
bloom or balloon or bomb—

dull shreds
in disarray on the dirt—
how modest their hiss
when all the air fled.

History's

tear coursed through our inelegant
wires. It darkened what had faded,
        mottled
the stiff ridge, trickled through
icy shackles;

hoarsened the language of chains, brining
our inmate-skin, rusting the fly-
screen, prowling the glass for faces

that kept slipping off.

It pooled under the grave-chinned stones
and grew a hood over the draped swan
and blackened the breast beating madly for a kiss.

It had no word for pistol or war. It was
the glistening aftermath. In its wake,
smoke guttered to steam.

The tear heavied the lash of the bull,
matted bear-hide, curled the page, swelled
the book where red print met blue—
resolving the world as blur.

A cold soak to our wistful meadow. We began
trailing its lucid tail, whereupon the tear

stretched its dumb cry and sidled through our skeletal
village. We could not unlock ourselves
for all its trembling glister,

its glinting spur too soft to do any more but course
and cool our anklebones, salting the root, not

reconciled with that fixed
smile of the world on which it dripped.

Carousel

The brutal white horses with painted-on faces
Are riding their circles, riding
Dead air. The dead air is hanging,
Is ridden with riders and glued-on red
Saddles. Crumpled hoofs in the dead-on air.

The wild glare of the brutal white horses
And the crippled gold manes tossing
Dead air and the two girls who ride them throwing
Their kisses from high, battered foreheads
Through the thin screams of their stringy red hair.

The brutal white horses are riding their circles,
Veering in terror from painted-on ropes
In dead-earnest air. The ropes that suspend them.
The brutal flare of their painted-in nostrils, the brutal
Whirl of their unfurling manes in the painted-on air.

Their paralyzed mouths the yellow bit snares,
Their petrified stares tapped by flies riding air
And they're riding in silence, glassed in
By air and the two girls who poke them
Dead in the eye and pound their fists on
The painted-on flanks are beginning to cry.

For the brutal white horses don't bolt or whinny, don't
Ever die, but ride their dead circles, noses on high,
The dead air upon them, the painted-on saddles
And painted-on reins, and painted-on lives. What mind
Would have them, circling and glassy, immune
And frozen in constant alarm.

Stephanie

The Mercury light went mute, faintly hooding
the parking lot. And inside,
strangers swiveling oblivious bar-room hips, laughter

like flecks, cold chips of ice tinkling far off while a man, abrupt,
hoarse, close to the root,
insistently, urgently names her *Stephanie Stephanie*

He will not take correction. His anonymous self will not take. *Stephanie*
Stephanie. The dirt beneath goes blank and blind
from the hit and thud—what's above won't register

raw push and grunt and push and
the scene begins again with what had been forgot:
he forces off the boot; he wrests the belt that had been
crying to be taken, moaning *Stephanie*

Stephanie in the dull leaves drained
flat like hearts.

It was winter, late autumn,
after someone somewhere had died. So cold the body
did not stop shuddering; shuddering became

the body's life. Like a moth. The mind dim,

dazedly wandering, now remembers
—the thin drift— *Stephanie Stephanie*
vacant—the loose skin of the dead

—exiled, the leaning tree and his soft white shirt falling
open like drawing room drapery or calla or amaryllis or mariposa lily—
will not stand correction. *Stephanie*

was this his call? Your answer?
Did you report?
[Took.]

Proximity

Still wet from its wild leap
out of the broken lake
it had no skull to speak of
but lay tremendous in the dust.

One heavy yellow eyelid
creased to a yolky flit,
a little, flattened hand poked out.

At first you were terrified
you'd crush it, your boot
sliding over its pus-stoppered throat.

You were afraid to bend near, afraid
to stoop and stroke its outline—
leaky with bogwater, hooded with sallow blood,

and then its crumpled body
in your palm, and then
who knew where that might lead?

By the low frog pond, in the listening twilight,
the urge to damage
what you could not rouse
did not lift.

Parade

Drink it all said maroon to red.
Bolster it up said navy to violet.
Git along, white said gray with a nudge that toppled
the snowdrift. *Plunge*
urged black of its tophat shadow.
Faintly darken around the edge screamed silver
in falsetto till it lost its voice.
Vanish implored translucent *varnish*.

They were well-meaning, coaxing
their counterparts towards the steep ledge.
They believed depth led to the soul. They thought
they had to fast-access it.

A Great Blue Heron turned on one Great Leg
A Russet Owl shivered in its Black-Eyed Hole

Canary yellow pecked a square of butter till they blurred
together and flew off, stained dandelion-bloom in beak.
(Green faintly smiled at this.)

And sleep, dear colorless, made its nightly cancellations.

How This Time the Moon

I

Moonlight is a hatchet that won't
pull out
of the blister-throated
bedside peony.

The ceramic vase turns cold
to its shadow. The chair-leg splits
from its oak. Faint sob
of a pillow in shafts.

A spackled woman severed from her blousy
button, a man unbuckled, striped like a belt.

The dust, aftermath
of bone, spins
to paralysis.

II

Moonlight is a pale hand
covering the faulty brows and lid,
placating the wrenched light of our factory.

It covers and stills
as necessary. Silk for the lake where the body floats.

Moon: hapless in your own light
severing and sleeving the earth, you are not
stopping the usual, terrible business.

Violence, the Word

I once found beautifully familiar.
Bruised chin-rest of the violin, gaunt
clef pinned to its corner.
Razor stirring in the basin.
The rope speaking quietly to a string.

These were quiet, hurt things.

In the shifting drift-horns of clouds,
the muttering trumpet of the east,
roads thinning to rivulets, fidgeting around
dead tufts of birds. Tambourines
blacked out and flutes leaked thin
blood from the mouth.

Then I could no longer let it into the house.

And when the bomb became an instrument,
I lost my singing lantern.
And I watched us take good care of the end—
spooning our sockets, piling dirt, hilling
earth to keep some curve to the planet, some
soft swell.

(The rest of the notes
were fugitive birds, flying swift,
tearing through the deadly staff.)

Blue Box

He's on hold, an edgy shovel.
The road's ploughed grit and dark again.

She's a doorway slit—
cold, nude, unwavering.

The yard's strewn with glittery strands and shreds,
tinseled hedge-lines, lit boas, blades.

Even at night—in that bright
corner—the eye hurts a little all the time.

A fifth of frost in the herbs.
The hardiest winter green shackled

by neck in ice. The red front
door a stop sign, hard

to determine. He stares like a diamond—studied and quick.
She kicks up the ice into crystal fur.

A wire dangles over the frozen hill—
a high-strung barb on which birds wait for a voice

to clap them awake. The clouds box fast
and spread thin. It is a blue and white

winter—a manageable Mary standing in a snowy grove,
a drained swan, a five-headed mouse with flat whiskers.

She has a dream about a shark edging near
a child's leg.

It must've been from the program she says
toward his head but it doesn't turn.

Some Footage

In the room, some stand like angels with hunched wings.
Some crumple roses in misfit smocks. Some smoke.

Some tilt toward his leveled tent and its dumbbell bone.
Some man a frantic lighthouse. Some tread. Some worm.

Some collapsed faces, some tight.
The inch-eyed stars don't want us in their light:

They stay us to the ground with pins. The cold bolts
for the count. The door's a wall.

His harrowed leg-clot. The black hole of his period
we can't peer through or stop. Some kiss the feet

of the dead, some kiss the skin until it turns porcelain and cracks,
some kiss the thin wrist as it turns iron, then soft, and rain rain.

III

In Memoriam: Lucy Grealy (1963-2002)

Here is the disembodied

voice of my friend & I think
of her in two places: one
in flickering violet strobes—
one in the bad man's sleek car, oh, & another
by the sea, wrapped blue & marigold, scarves loosening,

her skin the salt paper you'd wrap thin meat in,
stored near a cleaver, nudging the blade.

No matter how dangerously close she came
to light & man, each a knife against her cheek,
she didn't run lest she feel
the jiggling of her face re-patched.

Someone is always whispering
about me Lucy says deeply in my ear.
They must be angels, or harmonicas.

Lucy III

Your hands:
a pair of doves
in the snow, split
at the dull neck,
escaped from their circus.

Your green eyes gone yellow,
plugged,
swollen like bad milk.

Of the 39 yards of filament,
tendon, thread, those
thin strings
that move a body through

or hold it in suspension: your body
was the elemental color
of lament.

Your mouth—not
yours—a mouthing
of loneliness—a fissure

mutely inching toward
the jaw. Was
that the whole
trouble?

Quiet! This
afternoon is a folded
note, this after-
math, incalculable
news. We keep a hollow
ear on the bedstand and see
by fallen candle.

You were there in a yellow chair

You were there
in a yellow chair   I recite to the sand,
the speeding clouds, the bay.

A quiet wind lopes down the board-
walk on its halved heel, in dirty fur,
its wild forelock shakes, but cannot hide the face.

You were there
once, in a blue room   I chide the kite
slight on its unsteady stick
and its dreamy paunch-belly,
its fractured torso.

Its sister noses out to the silver sea
and tinselhood, light and curious,
like airblown gauze.

If only to assuage   I cry to the crow
who puts and pits and pitches its one wing.
If only for compass.

You won't have it. Your eye is bittern.
Your tongue—short shrift.

Breathing in so much
salt, you can bear to let it go.

Leave her,
sand, wind, kite, crow.

Public

I kept at it—finding
squares of light in envelopes
and then in boxes
alright, alright
until I found the book
she had become—left
splayed on the corner
of the YMCA rattle-
trap radiator.

It didn't perch as she had
when she was a human bird,
but lay face-up—defiant in fluorescence,
glossy even in its black
and hooded gray *alright, alright*

There it was—a dissolution
of threads and glue and inky strings
and the blocky prints of an animal
in snow, harmed, halting,
but determined against its own
collapse, while the binding gleamed
terribly, without teeth.

Send Lucy Downriver

Send Lucy downriver
She'll like the silk pull
a beautiful leaf

her thin face curled
the color of moss
shape of a rose
veiny and sweet, querulous, wise

She'll float the way all
leaves float

———

A small hiss
as you glide, little leaf
Brittle, you swim
where the world feels good—encircling,
swerving—your devoted partner
swirling your waist in the water

This is where you've turned, this is
where you've gone, haven't you?

Envoy

You kept a blue robe in a brown box.
The sky rested on a penny.
When you shut the lid, you made night
a memory of memory. Your bell
white-mouthed with music,

your redwing in arbor, your grazing azaleas, the pulse
of glittering leaves, the wind's ineluctable pull
into the mindful. You were predisposed to silence then

and climbed its sheer side and walked through the gravel, through
the glass door where the dark room waited
and all the errors in your life finally curled
around you, at your feet, their bristles flat,
their eyes gold with forgiveness.

Note—

When she was nine years old, Lucy Grealy was diagnosed with Ewing's Sarcoma, a form of cancer with a five percent survival rate. She lost nearly half her jaw to the disease, endured chemotherapy and years of painful operations.

About the Lena-Miles Wever Todd Poetry Series

The editors and directors of the Lena-Miles Wever Todd Poetry Series select one book of poems for publication by Pleiades Press and Winthrop University each year. All selections are made blind to authorship in an open competition for which any American poet is eligible.

. . . .

Other Books in the Series

Compulsions of Silkworms and Bees by Julianna Baggott (selected by Linda Bierds)

Snow House by Brian Swann (selected by John Koethe)

Motherhouse by Kathleen Jesme (selected by Thylias Moss)

Lure by Nils Michals (selected by Judy Jordan)

The Green Girls by John Blair (selected by Cornelius Eady)

A Sacrificial Zinc by Matthew Cooperman (selected by Susan Ludvigson)

The Light in Our Houses by Al Maginnes (selected by Betty Adcock)

Strange Wood by Kevin Prufer (selected by Andrea Hollander Budy)